Female: Experience, Strength, and Hope

For Monica —

A very special woman I've met along the journey.

Love,
Susan T.

Female: Experience, Strength, and Hope

Susan T.

Edited by Adam Shell

VANTAGE PRESS
New York

FIRST EDITION

Published by Vantage Press, Inc.
516 West 34th Street, New York, New York 10001

Manufactured in the United States of America
ISBN: 0-533-12282-1

Library of Congress Catalog Card No.: 97-90080

0 9 8 7 6 5 4 3 2 1

This book is dedicated to women.

Women who know shame.
Women who know fear.
Women who know loneliness.
Women who know courage.
Women who know risk.
Women who know truth.
Women who know passion.
Women who know women.

"What will I do if I stop drinking and drugging?
. . . everything else."

Contents

Foreword

Female: Experience, Strength, and Hope is a compilation of seven short stories about and dedicated to women. These real-life stories are written by women from all socioeconomic backgrounds who have suffered the anguish and pain of drug and alcohol abuse and later found the joy of recovery.

The mix of voices represented in the stories—black women, white women, a veteran Broadway dancer, a college professor, a musician, and women who learned life's lessons in America's inner cities—is powerful proof that substance abuse takes prisoners from every walk of life. The "voices" in this book are courageous voices, voices that will motivate others experiencing the hell of alcohol and drug abuse to muster up their own courage to get well.

In their own words, these seven remarkable women tell their private stories to the general public for the first time.

Adam Shell, Editor

Ruth's Story
(*This story is dedicated to my loving husband, Hector.*)

I was molested by a relative when I was four years old. He told me that he'd kill me if I told anyone. He even threatened to throw me out the window. On that day, fear was born. And, to this day, I'm still afraid of heights.

My name is Ruth. I'm a recovering alcoholic and drug addict.

I was born the fourth of my father's seventeen children. I was raised by a stepmother because my father threw my mother out when I was a baby and never let her see us. (I met my real mother for the first time when I was in high school.) I remember once sitting on my father's lap. I remember it because it was the only time I received any type of affection from him.

I never felt like I belonged, so I became a people pleaser. I wanted to be all things to all people. I would go to any lengths for people not to get mad at me; I wanted everyone to like me.

I lived in fear, too. In school, I was always afraid that the teacher would call on me. I would break out in a sweat if she looked my way. It wasn't that I didn't know the answer, I just didn't like being put on the spot. I was afraid of making a mistake and being laughed at. Being the tallest girl in the class didn't help, either. I remember the shortest girl in school slapped me in front of everyone, and I did nothing. I feel the shame to this day. Everyone, even my family, never let me forget it. They didn't understand how fear could paralyze a person. My fear continued to grow because my father was prone to angry outbursts. Without much warning, he would lash out at my step-mother or one of us kids. My life became a living hell. I would have bad dreams about death.

And I wet the bed until I was ten, the same age I got my first period. I was so scared because I didn't know what was happening to my body. I thought it was my fault. I started to hide my blood-stained underclothes so nobody would find out. When my stepmother finally found out, she told me to talk to my older sister, who would tell me what to do.

Since I had developed early in life, men began to notice me and whistle. Again, I thought I had done something wrong. I would run all the way home with my heart beating out of my chest. Everything was just so confusing.

Things got worse when I was sixteen.

I met a boy who lived down the street. He never made any disrespectful remarks toward me, so I trusted him. One day he asked me to go to his grandmother's house with him to pick up something. My father had gone down south for my uncle's funeral, so I said okay.

That was my darkest day.

I was raped.

I was scared. I was in pain. I felt lost. I was humiliated and ashamed. I had no place to go, no one to talk to. I was so terrified that I didn't tell anyone for days.

The rapist had beat me up, but my real pain was inside.

I couldn't escape. This boy, this monster, kept harassing me. I needed help, so I told this guy I liked—some guy who wanted to be my boyfriend—what happened. He was very understanding and we started going out. He understood that I didn't want to get close to him or any other guy because I didn't trust anyone. The next time the rapist knocked on my door, my boyfriend answered. I never saw the rapist again.

My boyfriend (whom, by the way, I ended up marrying seven years later) was nice, but he used drugs. We broke up when he got arrested and went to jail.

When I graduated from high school, I left home and moved to the south. That's where I learned to drink.

Down south, real drinkers don't use shot glasses. If you want to drink, you have to buy your own moonshine and gulp it down straight from the bottle. I learned to drink with the best of them. After heavy drinking binges, I would come home with black eyes, bruises, and, sometimes, no shoes. I started to have blackouts, but I didn't even know it.

I wasn't used to alcohol and after awhile, my body simply shut down. I couldn't get out of bed for two weeks. My dress size went from fourteen to seven. I called my sister and told her I was sick. My stepmother sent me a non-refundable plane ticket to New Jersey. When I got back to Jersey, I stayed with my sister and her family. I got a job, but couldn't stop drinking. I was tormented by my past. My sister would wake me from my nightmares in the middle of the night.

I was overly sensitive. I was hurt. I was rebellious. I was angry. I felt tremendous rage.

And I was always looking for a fight. I started threatening my brother-in-law's friends to the point where they wouldn't let their wives hang out with me anymore. I didn't think I was doing anything wrong. Everybody got drunk sometimes, didn't they?

I was young. I had no kids. I was living the life of a swinging single. All my money was my money. I figured I'd do whatever the hell I wanted to do.

A few months later, I decided it was time to get married. First, I had to find a husband. The problem was I had no idea how to pick one. One thing I knew, though, was that my future husband had to wear white socks. (Isn't it insane to pick a man by the color of his socks?) I had heard somewhere that men who wore white socks made good husbands because they weren't streetwise.

I ended up dating a bus driver who wore white socks as part of his uniform. From the start, the relationship was built on lies. I don't even remember liking him. I got pregnant and asked him to make an honest woman out of me. But instead of putting a ring on my finger, he told me that he was already married. I went crazy. He kept telling me that he would marry me in two years, that he just needed time to break up with his wife. I didn't have two years. Hell, no!

During the months I was carrying my son, my drinking increased. Every time I took a drink, my son would kick inside my belly. I thought it was funny. At the time, I didn't know anything about the effects alcohol has on the fetus.

After I gave birth to my son, my feelings were dead. The baby's father got mad because I didn't name the boy after him. He left. I didn't see him for years.

I went through all the pains of childbirth alone. My father was ashamed and wanted nothing to do with me. When I went into labor and needed a ride to the hospital, my stepmother said she had to go to work. My sister called me a cab. Nobody visited me in the hospital. I was angry and depressed. I didn't even see my baby until it was time to go home.

When I got home, I had little to do with the baby. My sister took care of him. My child even slept in her room. Then one night my baby got sick. I panicked. I held him while two friends ran to the drugstore and got some medicine. That night, for the first time, I bonded with my son. He got better, but I was getting sicker.

I was drinking again and taking pills. I couldn't stop. I spent my days sitting on the steps in front of the house laughing, talking, and gossiping.

Then I bumped into my old boyfriend from high school again, the one who had gone to jail. We hit it off. We lived together for two years and then got married. He was my friend. He loved my son and took him everywhere. After we got married, he stopped doing drugs.

But I was still uptight. At my husband's suggestion, I started smoking pot to help me relax. I didn't really like it, but I did it anyway. On weekends, my sister-in-law and I would leave our kids with my husband and go to the bars and drink. I would only drink one shot of gin with my pills when we went out because I knew that Marilyn Monroe had died from mixing booze and pills. I didn't want to die like she did.

I finally quit taking pills when I got a job as a barmaid. Booze became my best friend again. I partied every night at work; the music sounded better. If I got drunk enough, things didn't seem so bleak. But when I got home, the bed would spin, which I hated. One night I left with some guy I met at the bar and almost went to bed with him. But the memories of being raped at sixteen filled my head and frightened me. I was scared, but took a risk and said "no." It worked. The guy understood that no meant no. Thank God. I went home and found out that my husband had been out looking for me. I told him the truth. He believed me when I told him I hadn't slept with the guy from the bar. He truly loved me.

But love wasn't enough. My husband started shooting up heroin again. He was selling drugs, too. He always wanted the best for me, but drugs always came first. Finally, he ended up in jail again. I visited him on weekends. Then one day I decided that I didn't want to be one of those women whose highlight of the week was to visit a lawbreaker in prison.

I got off welfare. I got a job working in the school system. Part of my job was monitoring the students in the halls between classes. As soon as they went to class, I would sneak into the bathroom and snort cocaine. It wasn't my drug of choice, but it was free. The guys I worked with gave it to me. I met people on the job, including my supervisors, who were breaking the law every day. Hanging around with the wrong crowd at work eventually got me into trouble a few years later. I was indicted on seventeen counts of forgery. I really was innocent. I did sign checks, but I didn't know that they were made out to deceased co-workers. Out of sixty-three people, only two of us were set free. I was one of them.

Next, I went to work for a juvenile corrections center. It didn't take long before I fell in with the counselors who drugged. I didn't need to leave the building to get high—most of the counselors used and sold drugs at work.

At that time, I started going out with a man thirty years older than I was. He had money and for the first time in my life, I was living in the lap of luxury. We bought a house that was decorated by professionals. I was driving a Lincoln Town Car and traveling to the islands several times a year. I thought I had it all.

I was still young and impressionable. Plus, he let me do what I wanted. He approved of my drinking and cocaine use. I had also developed a heroin habit while working at the correctional facility, which started a twelve-year affair with The Devil. But he didn't know how bad my heroin addiction was. I was too good at covering my tracks. I can't go into detail about my dance with The Devil because the anger and pain would overtake me. Just let me say that it's sad that I let myself be so belittled. Finally, I broke up with my male friend. I know now that I did it so I could drug more. After eight years, I was free once again. Now I could do all the drugs I wanted without having to answer to anyone.

I quickly lost control. I started carrying a gun in a shoulder holster. I sold drugs for a while. I was stabbed. I was kidnaped. Sometimes I went hungry. All my money went for drugs.

My son went through hell. He had no mother. He didn't have a father, either. He was raising himself. When he was eleven, I got real depressed for about a month, and he had to take care of himself and me. I was oblivious to everything. I focused on only one thing: my addiction. We moved about five or six times a year. I thought that was normal. At one place we lived, I was such an outcast that the kids on the block threw rocks at me. My son got into a lot of fights. *Is it because of me?* I wondered. I would send him over to my sister's house to eat when he was hungry. I was hungry, too, I hurt for him. Today, he's a very angry young man.

When I turned thirty-five, I thought I had had enough. The truth is I ran out of money. My father had a terrible accident that year. He fell off the roof of the local church and was in pretty bad shape. The doctors didn't think he'd walk again. But, praise God, he did. During a visit to the hospital, he pleaded with me and my sister to get help. I promised him that I would find someone to help me beat my addiction if my family life didn't get any better. After our talk I went out and got high. When I came back to the hospital to visit him, he saw me in the raw. He saw me in a way he never had before. So did my sisters and everyone else in the hospital. I didn't know how bad I acted until my father went up for his operation and my sisters started laughing about all the things I had said and done. I didn't remember a thing. I was in a blackout. I felt ashamed and wondered what other embarrassing things I had done that I didn't remember.

I realized, then, that I needed professional help. I called a help line, and the counselor who took the call got me into a rehab that fit my specifications. After all, I didn't just lay my hat anywhere. I asked the older guy I used to date to bring me drugs. He did, but I changed my mind and didn't take them. It didn't matter because the rehab threw me out for breaking the rules anyway. It turns out my friend told the counselors that I asked for drugs. I couldn't understand why he turned me in. Then I figured it out. He knew that if I got straight, I wouldn't need him anymore.

I left the rehab and went directly across the street to a bar and started drinking again. I wanted to get back at the counselors and wanted them to see me getting wasted; nobody was even watching. After a few drinks, I got a ride to my favorite bar and spent the rest of the night drinking and telling everyone how to stay sober. The rest of the night I was in a blackout. I don't remember that night or much of the next month for that matter. But I do remember running into the counselor who had checked me into the rehab a few weeks earlier. Of course, I was high. He gave me the number of an AA contact. I called her, but she depressed me. She told me about a rehab that had helped her. I didn't follow through.

One night, not long after that, I was broke and going crazy. I looked around the house trying to find something that would help me go to sleep. I wanted time to hurry up so that it could be the next day. All I could find was a bottle of Anacin. It didn't help. My heart started beating fast, my ears were ringing, and I sat up all night. I was really scared. I was shaking uncontrollably. I thought I was mentally ill. The next day I contacted the counselor who got me into the first rehab. She immediately took me to a rehab at a nearby hospital. I didn't care that someone I knew might see me. I just needed help.

By the time I got to the hospital, some of the hysteria had worn off, and I was beginning to feel cocky again. I tried to postpone treatment for a few days, but the nurse gave me an ultimatum to be there at ten the next morning. I told her I'd be there. I left, got my welfare check, bought some heroin, and used all I could without overdosing. Since I had to be there by 10:00 A.M., I rushed home at 9:10 A.M. to pack my clothes, all of which were dirty. I snorted my last bag of heroin on the steps of the hospital. I didn't think it was a big deal if I overdosed because I was already at the hospital. Pretty smart, huh. I was in a blackout by the time I got to the detox unit.

Let me describe how I looked when I arrived at the hospital after staying out all night doing drugs. I had my wig on. My false eyelashes had started to peel off. My face was smudged with lipstick. I tried to put it on, but I got it on my chin and forgot to wipe it off. I wore spike heels and a suit. My clothes were packed in a suitcase with wheels. I had taken great pains in dressing because I wanted to make a big entrance. After all, the first impression is the lasting impression, right?

I was paranoid and suspicious of the staff and the other clients. The staff let me stay in bed for two days. I was that out of it. By the time I came out of my blackout, the other clients hated me. Of course, I didn't know why. But, as time went on, I started to make some friends. I became curious about how this thing—sobriety—works. It was weird that the people who came to speak to us didn't appear to be weighed down with so many feelings. I had always suffered from jagged feelings that cut and hurt me. I wanted to feel like them. I was confused a lot of the time. I couldn't figure out why. Then one day a speaker said to me: "You look like you need something." He then handed me a copy of the "Twelve Promises" of AA. The promises spelled out everything I had been searching for in my life. I began to ask questions. How can I get to where they are? I was told that I had to be honest, open, and willing. Okay, I can do that. I also wanted to know how to rid myself of the obsession to pick up a drink or sniff a line. A counselor on the floor said, "Pray for it to be removed." I wasn't so sure that praying would be enough. I had always been a "praying" addict. The counselor said to this, "Ask and it shall be given." I didn't believe him, but I was willing to give it a try.

Every night, while my roommate slept, I prayed. Two months later, I found that my obsession had been removed, never to return. It was that simple.

Praise God. I did not complicate things. I kept it real simple. I already believed in God, so it wasn't hard to accept the spirituality of the program. The first night they told me to make meetings. And I did. I would come early, sit up front, empty ashtrays, and stay late. People would watch me. I got a job two weeks after I got out of treatment. I was scared most of the time. Everything was so new to me. I had never tried to live by any rules except my own. It was too hard. Everything I tried to do seemed to turn out wrong. But, after a few weeks of meetings and working the program, I started to listen to suggestions from other people. I didn't try to do a lot of "thinking" because my "best thinking" got me in trouble. I made my ninety meetings in ninety days. And ninety after that. And ninety more after that. I wanted some insurance that I would not go back to my old ways. It wasn't until my second year in the program that I began to see how sick I really was.

At that time, I started to work in a rehab. I liked it. My son graduated from high school, moved to Buffalo, and got a job in Canada. I started going with a new guy. I had not had a relationship in two years. I didn't know whether to hold hands or kiss on the first date. I felt like a teenager all over again. When we broke up, it was very hard. It was like losing a first love.

My sister died after I entered the program. She had been to a rehab twice. She just didn't get it. It was hard on all of us.

I got to know a guy I met in the program. I liked him. So when he and his girlfriend broke up, I asked him out. We fell in love and decided to get married. First, we bought a house and planned our wedding for a whole year. Our wedding was perfect, just perfect. My family respected him. We went on our honeymoon and settled down when we got home. We decided to go on a cruise and paid for it ahead of time. (The future looked bright.) Unfortunately, my husband had been sick off and on for a few years. He hated hospitals and felt that if he went to the hospital he wouldn't return. He got sicker and wouldn't see a doctor until I insisted. I took him to the hospital and a week later he died from liver disease. It was a terrible way to die. My husband was a recovering alcoholic, too. He had been sober for twelve years. Before getting sober, he used to drink cheap wine. We were married just nine months, but had been together more than five years. For that I feel blessed.

I loved him. I am going through a lot of grief and loss, but I don't want to "use." I know the pain will pass. But right now, I hurt.

Since my husband's death, I earned my counseling certification and am seeking another. He would be proud of me. I look forward to setting new goals and achieving them. The hopes that were born in rehab more than ten years ago are still shining in my heart. I'm thankful for following through on something—going to meetings, getting a sponsor, joining a group, and getting active.

It's a good life.

Claudia's Story

Success, fame, fortune. It appeared I had it all. But I was missing one thing: me. Who was I? I was a drunk.

I always said I would never become a heavy drinker, but that's exactly what I became—despite an exhilarating eight-year run as a lead dancer in a hit Broadway musical. Why did I become a verbally, emotionally, and mentally abusive alcoholic?

I started my ballet training when I was seven. I was very talented, and my parents were proud of me when I was dancing. I got the attention and validation I needed by becoming the best dancer. And I was. I loved to dance. I was passionate about dance. I had a world to call my own.

I began drinking when I was twelve. I started with beer, then I graduated to marijuana. I briefly quit dancing when I was fifteen. That's when I became interested in drinking and guys. I was an alcoholic by the time I was seventeen. I was a daily drunk for ten years. I could not stop for one day. I believed that my purpose in life, the purpose God had given me, was to drink, and I had surrendered to this fact.

I was born to drink. I thought I would probably die at a young age, but that was okay. It was my destiny. I also knew I would never have children because I would have to stop drinking if I was to carry a child, and I was not willing to stop drinking. You see, my sense of responsibility was warped. I remember thinking that if my liver went bad, I would just get a liver transplant. And once I received the transplant, I would pick up with my drinking where I left off. This thinking was totally insane. But what was more insane is what I was willing to sacrifice to continue drinking. I didn't think I would ever get married. I figured the only person who would want to marry a drunk would be a fellow drunk, and that wasn't good enough for me.

During all this time, my career was going great. At eighteen, I decided to go into musical theater. I traveled around the world, did some commercials, a few films, and got my first Broadway show when I was twenty-one. I got my second Broadway show when I was twenty-five. I had a featured role that required extreme physical energy and mental and emotional strength. But all I could think of was drinking.

The first thought that came to mind every morning was: I can't wait to start drinking. My favorites were white wine and vodka, but I'd drink anything. I always made sure I had enough in the house, so when I got home from work, I could start drinking. I looked at alcohol as courses of a meal. My entrée was a half gallon of wine. For dessert I had a pint of vodka with a splash of orange or cranberry juice.

I started plunging deeper and deeper toward my bottom. I was missing a lot of work, and when I was out on stage, I was shaking, salivating, ready to pass out, and very paranoid. I told my stage manager I was sick and had to go home. Nobody had any idea what was going on. I had gastritis and bronchitis on and off. I kept relapsing with bronchitis and became hooked on codeine, too.

During this time, I was involved in a bunch of horrible relationships. I just wanted someone to love me. Much of my story is very painful, so painful and sickening, in fact, that while I was getting set to write about my failed relationships, I got physically ill and wanted to vomit. I had to stop writing.

We all have war stories. I will not share them here because we all know what they're like. I can only say that there must have been someone looking out for me, knowing I had another purpose in life, because I should have been dead. It's amazing that I'm here writing this story.

Anyway, I started becoming aware that I was getting closer and closer to the end. I remember my father's fiftieth birthday surprise party. I was drunk. But I heard something that day that made me want to change. My father was preaching about the importance of education. I had never gone to college, but through my drunkenness, I heard his words. I knew I couldn't do it if I was drunk, but deep inside I knew I wanted a college degree.

This was the turning point. Five days later I called AA at 3:00 A.M. and asked where a meeting was the next day. The next day was Saturday, and I didn't make it. I drank instead. The next night I called AA again, but on Sunday I drank again. On Monday, I knew the end was near. I was sick with bronchitis. I called in sick to work. I went to my parents' house and spoke to my father. You see, my father had been "Twelve Stepped" fifteen years earlier, and I knew I had seen the "Twenty-Four Hour A Day" book lying around the house. I told him I had a problem with alcohol, that I couldn't stop but wanted to stop, I needed to go to AA. He supported my decision. Off I went to get a refill of my codeine prescription, then over to a bar that my friend worked at. I had some wine and went home. I was totally smashed. I continued drinking at home. And I believe that then came my spiritual awakening, and was what got me into the rooms of AA.

I was drinking my vodka and reading Betty Ford's book, *A Glad Awakening*, which chronicles the former

First Lady's bout with alcoholism. It was difficult to read because everything was so blurry, but I was trying. At the same time, the TV program *Cagney and Lacey* was on. Now, I don't watch this show, so I don't even know who was who, but I do remember the blonde character saying, "My name is ——— and I'm an alcoholic." I looked up from the book and turned to the TV. She was standing before an AA meeting admitting her alcoholism. It wasn't a coincidence; it was fate. It was like God was putting these things before me.

At that moment I cried out to God for help. "Please help me. I can't stand it anymore." I felt like I was shackled in hell, a lonely, dying hell. And, you know, God heard me and came into my hell. I never thought of God being in hell, only heaven, but God came into my hell and sat and talked with me. I calmed down enough to finally go to sleep, but somehow I knew it was going to be okay.

When I awoke the miracle had occurred. Yes, God had carried me out of hell. I was no longer stuck. I knew what I was to do. I felt reborn. I was not religious, but something changed my life that night. It was God.

I got up. The AA meeting was at 1:00 P.M. I put on a skirt. (I never wear skirts, but I wanted to look presentable.) I got in my car. I was scared, and never drove as slowly as I did on my way to that first meeting. I walked in a little late. It was a small meeting. The four things I remember hearing were: "Don't pick up the first drink and you can't get drunk" (Wow! What a concept! How come I never thought of that?); "ninety meetings in ninety days" (which I did); "stay away from men and stick with the women"; and "get a sponsor."

I shared at the meeting. I was shaking. I introduced myself as an alcoholic. Remarkably, the woman who would be my sponsor was at that first meeting. I left feeling like a new woman, like a weight had been lifted off my shoulders. I thought that if I just stopped drinking my whole life would be normal.

That first twenty-four hours I did not have a drink and thought the obsession had been lifted. Mind you, I had been drunk every day for ten years. I was so excited about going twenty-four hours without a drink that I called my mother and told her. This was, I thought, a very great accomplishment. I wasn't one to tell anybody, just my family. It was my own secret triumph. But, believe me, I wanted to shout it from the rooftops. I wanted to stand in the middle of the stage—on Broadway—and shout it to the audience, to shout my joy of sobriety and my new life. But I just smiled inside and kept it to myself.

I was immediately on a pink cloud, which lasted about one year. I got a sponsor about one month into the program. I remember thinking, *I hope she says yes, that she'll be my sponsor.* I believe I chose her because my soul was drawn to her. It took me one year to call her. I called her when I started experiencing pain and my character defects started to come out. My sponsor, who to this day, eight years later, is still my sponsor, saved my life a number of times. I call her my angel. She is one of the most important, if not the most important, tools in my recovery.

My second and third years of sobriety were very painful. I was in a relationship, of course, and found all kinds of issues and defects coming up. I did not trust. I was suspicious. I was jealous. I was controlling, demanding, and obsessive. It was like I had taken a prisoner. I verbally, emotionally, and mentally attacked my boyfriend. I was mean and cruel. But underneath was a wounded, scared, insecure, hurt, sad woman with low self-esteem. I didn't know how to talk about it. Actually, I was embarrassed to let anybody really know what was going on inside of me. I just wasn't ready for a relationship. So I went a year without a man, and it was a great year. See, being with a boyfriend really pushes my triggers. This year gave me time to look at, and work on, myself. In the fifth year, I was in a horrible relationship with a man I met in the program. The torment I felt that year made me think I might as well be drinking. And God knows I wanted to drink, but somehow I believe that I was saying good-bye to the old me. It had its purpose.

After five years, I was ready to do my first fourth step—I conducted a moral inventory of myself. I knew this was another big turning point. I would go to my sponsor's house and write for about an hour each day. Two weeks later I was done. Next, I did my fifth step: I shared the contents of my moral inventory with my sponsor and burned it in the fireplace. I told her things that were embarrassing, but she never invalidated or judged me. Actually, she shared some of her own stuff. We got closer that day and I felt new. I was finally ready for a new life.

I met my husband-to-be at work. We developed a friendship and gradually fell in love. But, once again, I felt my defects rearing up. Fortunately for me, attacking and destructive behavior was not acceptable to him. This was another turning point in my recovery. A noted author calls this a "conversion experience." I was not willing to live my life without him, so I had to change. I spent a week at Hazelden, a Minnesota renewal center for recovering alcoholics and drug addicts. I had been going there once or twice a year for a number of years. I went there this time with a purpose and came back with my plan to change. And I did. I battled daily with my defects. It was a civil war going on inside of me. I did something different and it worked.

Today, my life is so very different. I'm married to that

man. He's the most wonderful man I've ever met. I graduated from college and plan on going back for my master's degree. I moved to the West Coast and now earn my living working with animals. My family relationships are healing. I'm no longer in show business, but it will probably always be part of my life. I'm sober. I'm free. I have hope. I experience serenity. I laugh. I cry. I play. I live. I belong to a women's spiritual group. I have the best sponsor (and friend) in the whole world. My home is safe and loving. I'm living a life I could never have imagined. It's beyond my wildest dreams.

I know what I have to do: go to meetings, talk to my sponsor, meditate, pray, empower and be empowered by other women, don't pick up that first drink, go to Hazelden, talk, share, feel, hope, allow my feelings, heal, and know that I didn't do this by myself. A power greater than myself is working in my life and I'm grateful. Sobriety is the most precious gift. I must never forget it was given to me.

I will take good care of this gift.

God Bless!

Bernice's Story

I'm an only child. My mother and father were both alcoholics. My father left when I was a baby, so my mother raised me alone.

Mom liked to "party." However, what she and her friends referred to as partying back in the '50s and '60s is called "drinkin' and druggin' " today. Besides drinking, my mother also had rules that governed her household. The problem was that the rules seemed to apply only to me. I didn't like that, and vowed early in life, when I was still a kid, to get out as quickly as possible. But it's hard for a child to just pick up and go. Until I was old enough to walk out the door of my mother's house and make it on my own, I found escape in my imagination. I created a safe, wonderful world I lovingly called "Barbie Land."

In real life, though, things weren't so wonderful. We lived in small quarters and moved frequently. I never had my own bedroom, just a single bed in the living room where my uncle or a friend of the family also slept. To get away from what seemed like a never-ending party, I created a pink-and-white world; Barbie was white, her furniture was pink. It was a world where I wasn't bothered by adults' drinking, smoking, laughing, crying, fighting, and cursing. My entire world was in the hallway near the front door. Occasionally, someone would open the door too wide and destroy my world. But I shrugged it off and told Barbie that we lived in California. I lived in "Barbie Land" until I was twelve. That's when I discovered boys.

At the time, I was lonely. I resented the fact that I didn't have a daddy and wanted to escape. So I set out to find the perfect man to take me away from my painful life. I dreamed of what it would be like when I got married. I had it all planned. We would have two kids (a boy first and then a girl), a house with a backyard, and a brown puppy named Scruffy and a kitten named Muffy. I searched all over for my man. Unfortunately, looking all over wasn't exactly what it sounds like. The truth is I couldn't leave my block, so the pickin's were mighty slim. Then one day, when I least expected it, I spotted him. He was down at the end of the block by the vacant building, breaking more windows than any of the other boys. I was impressed. He also held the record for cursing, drinking beer, cutting school, and beating people up. He was from Newark, too. That cinched it. Here was my way out of Orange.

At age fifteen and still a virgin, I was introduced to his version of sex. Rape is probably a better word. But I had an agenda, and no amount of physical pain could outweigh my determination to get out, to be free, to not end up like my mother. Despite the abuse, we married Islam fashion, moved around the corner, and had two kids (a boy first then a girl). But that's where the dream ended and my nightmare began. At age twenty, after a zillion black eyes, broken noses, and sexually transmitted diseases, it occurred to me that things were not going the way I had planned. My husband and I split up for good.

I got my own apartment and with it came freedom, which I had never experienced before. I liked it.

Now, about this partying thing. I had no idea that it was a skill I was to master until it mastered me. Since I had the misfortune of only having sex with one person who didn't know it was to be agreed upon by both parties, I wasn't interested in doing it ever again, except to procreate. However, I soon learned that alcohol not only loosens lips, it loosens hips, too. When I drank Southern Comfort with a twist of lemon, I became Mae West, Honey West, and Orange's best all rolled into one. Sex was fun. Hell, life was fun.

When I was twenty-five, I had another baby boy. Seventeen days later my mother died. Then I found cocaine and I felt as if my life was really going to get better—"right after this hit." I began to move frequently, mostly when the rent was due. Because of my ability to manipulate the system and men, the kids and I lived in most of the better apartments in the area. But things got progressively worse as I searched for what was missing in my life. Exactly what that something was, I don't know. But the truth is, by this time I could not have stopped abusing drugs and alcohol if I had wanted to. Partying was my life, just as it was my mom's life.

There was, however, one big difference between me and my mom: She made it to work every day whether she was drunk or not. At the end, the only work I could find was in the sex industry. We were living in the cutest house with a bedroom for everyone, a backyard, a finished basement, and a bathroom so big you could fit a bed in it. The rent, thanks to the government, was seventeen dollars per month. The rent each month was less than an hour's pay. The sex trade pays pretty good. Yet, I could not hold on to the money I made long enough to pay my landlord. He threw me out. The eviction notice was for thirty-four dollars. On "E Day" I threw a moving party, not that I had bothered to find another apartment. It was just a good excuse to have a party. The kids were outside playing—at least the eleven- and-twelve-year-old were. The six-year-old was home with his daddy who had left the situation a long time ago. Anyway, the constable came and padlocked my door. And I again said to myself: Things aren't going the way I planned.

Lucky for me, some guy came riding up on a motorcycle and offered me a ride. I saw him as my knight in shining armor on a white horse, so I said yes. After a couple of days, "Mr. Sweets" would no longer supply my habit and I began to come out of what I know today was a blackout. The last thing I could remember was being in front of my padlocked door, the kids outside playing, and wondering where we would all sleep that night. I then started wondering about more important things, like where the next hit was coming from. Then it hit me. I screamed out loud: "Where are the kids!?" No one heard me because I happened to be in "Sweets' " abandominium, and he wasn't home.

I didn't know where or how to find help, so I called the Division of Youth and Family Services, told them my kids were outside playing, and asked if they would go to the street and pick them up. I also told them I was going to kill myself and wouldn't be able to take care of them anymore. Fortunately, they had been contacted a week earlier by a family member. It turns out my kids, instead of waiting for me to come back, had the good sense to go the relatives after I drove off with Sweets. Good thing, because I didn't come back for 156 hours.

I was thirty-one when I entered recovery. My experience in detox was enough to get me and everyone else at the "Stinkin' Lincoln"—the neighborhood "get-high" hotel—sober. I didn't know about people, places, and things. When I went into rehab, I had matching luggage—two

Shop-Rite bags. Inside the bags I had all the drug paraphernalia I thought they would teach us to use properly; I didn't want to share anyone's equipment or wait for it. Instead, I got three hots and a cot. They taught me to wear undergarments again. They told me I could take off my wool kangol and wash and comb my hair. They told me I didn't kill my mother. They said that she was human and made mistakes, and that I could separate the terrible things she did from the person she was when she was sober. They told me it was all right to dislike the things my mother did and still love her. Whew, it was deep. I learned how to pray again, and my higher power told me that I was forgiven. My sponsor gave me my ninety-day pin and a hug. I was richer than I ever dreamed. After a while I got custody of the kids, made a lot of meetings, went back to school, made a lot of meetings, got a job, made a lot of meetings, and prayed a lot.

This program promises continued sobriety if you follow their directions. The rest is gravy. I'm living proof. Today, I'm living Barbie's dream. Through the program I met and married the man of my dreams. We own our home, my daughter is in her third year of college, my oldest son graduated high school and joined the navy, and my youngest son hasn't killed anyone yet. All in all, we are truly blessed. They told me "in order to keep it, you have to give it away." Well, please accept this humble offer of my story so that I may keep what I have learned to love and cherish: my sobriety. 7–18–88.

Susan's Story

Anxiety. Some people say they don't know which came first, the anxiety or the drinking, because each one can cause the other. But, in my case, I know very well which came first: anxiety.

I went from a very light social drinker to a full-blown alcoholic in less than one year. Here is my story.

I was thirty-six years old. Divorced for more than a year after a very difficult twelve-year marriage, I was living with my two daughters, aged four and seven, in a lovely home, in a lovely town. To make ends meet, I cared for other people's children in my house and rented one of my bedrooms to a businesswoman. I had a supportive family living in another state and wonderful friends and neighbors. Although there were worries, mainly over money, I was happy and content to live my life alone with my daughters. I never wanted to marry again.

My marriage had been too emotionally painful. My husband was the child of a violent, alcoholic father with whom he had a love-hate relationship. His mother was loving, but passive and meek. Although my husband didn't have a problem with alcohol, he did have a problem with anger. He would have uncontrollable outbursts of rage. Most of the time, his rage was directed at me. I spent my marriage, up until the last year, trying to figure out how to fix him. I finally realized (after he began to direct some of his irrational behavior toward our daughters) that I couldn't fix him. I also decided that I would not allow him to mistreat my daughters. I couldn't bear the thought of my two little girls growing up under his sick influence. I saw firsthand the effects of his father's behavior on his family, and I knew that I didn't want this pattern to continue with my children.

Looking back, it's interesting that the thought of leaving him didn't occur to me until his behavior started to impact my children directly. I wasn't able to muster up the courage to end the marriage simply because he was mistreating me. There must have been something lacking in me to allow him to emotionally abuse me for so many years. Something prevented me from leaving. When I would reach the breaking point and threaten to leave, he would promise me that he would change and would beg for just one more chance. I desperately wanted to believe him, but nothing ever changed. It only got worse. His behavior was like Dr. Jekyll and Mr. Hyde. At times he could be very loving, fun, and display a wonderful sense of humor. Other times he was vicious. His rages were normally followed by weeks of punishing silence. I became comfortable in the silence.

I am Irish, Catholic, the second oldest of five children. Neither my parents, grandparents, nor siblings are alcoholic. I was raised very strictly in a home where you were punished if you broke the rules. Opinions and feelings were never discussed. Period. My brothers and sisters and I were obedient, responsible, and well mannered. It never occurred to us to behave any other way. We never shared our anger, fear, or sadness. It was a family that suffered from great emotional deprivation. There was little connectedness, even among us kids. My father deserted us when I was twelve years old. My mother, deeply heartbroken, never told her three youngest children that he was gone. This is a perfect example of how I was raised. Don't talk about it, don't feel it, just go on as if everything were okay.

I was married just before I turned twenty-three. My husband and I met at work and married two years later. We had an active social life. I drank socially and got drunk occasionally. I had fun with alcohol, but felt no dependency at all. Alcohol, however, did not agree with me physically. I got terrible hangovers from drinking, much more so than my friends. It would take me a few days to feel completely well again after getting drunk.

My older sister died of cancer three weeks after my marriage. Although I regularly visited her in the hospital, the reality of her condition was never discussed in the family. Her death was a powerful trauma for me.

Two years after her death, I became claustrophobic. I had never experienced anything like it before. It was terrifying. What's worse, my husband was totally unsympathetic. I finally went to a psychiatrist, at the suggestion of my mother, and he put me on Tofranil for a year. The claustrophobia didn't go away, but it was nice to have someone to talk to and be listened to. I had never had my feelings validated before. My husband was very threatened by my seeing the psychiatrist, and I abruptly quit because I couldn't bear having it thrown in my face any longer. I never really discussed my relationship with my husband with the doctor. During the balance of my marriage, I continued to suffer from bouts of anxiety and claustrophobia. I occasionally took Valium, but most often felt secure enough just knowing I had the Valium in case I needed it. My husband ridiculed me for my fears and anxieties. My first daughter was born when I was twenty-seven, and the second when I was thirty. During all of these years, up until and through my divorce, I was a very light social drinker. Alcohol just didn't agree with me that much, and I didn't really care about it. I had also noticed that if my anxiety was bad, alcohol seemed to make it worse, so I didn't drink when I felt anxious.

During all of this time, I was smoking a pack of Newports every day. I felt that cigarettes were my best friend. They were always there to help me get through the bad times and share the good times. My mother was always encouraging me to quit smoking. She even offered me a thousand dollars to stop. I didn't take her up on her offer. As much as I could have used the money, cigarettes were more important to me. At the time, I remember thinking, *If they just wanted me to never drink again, that would be so easy—but not cigarettes.*

Thirteen months after my divorce, a good friend of mine was having a big fortieth birthday party for herself. She insisted that I get a date, but I didn't want one. But she was determined to find someone for me, regardless of what I thought. A friend of hers knew a very eligible bachelor. The necessary calls were made, and a blind date was arranged. It was one week before the party. The man was described as very popular, very successful, handsome, a few years older than I was, single, no children. In other words, "the ideal man."

I agreed to meet him for lunch at his club.

It was a Sunday in late January 1983. I walked in, we shook hands (he seemed nice), and we went to our table. As soon as we sat down, I began to shake all over. It was an anxiety attack like I had never experienced before. I had dated a couple of other men after my divorce without any problems. My date said, "You seem to have caught a chill coming in." I could not stop the shaking. It got worse and worse. It got so bad that I excused myself and went into the ladies' room, but when I came back, the shaking started all over again. It was the most embarrassing moment of my life. I wished the earth would open up and swallow me. My date kept chatting as if I were normal and suggested we have a drink to help me get rid of my chill. I ordered a glass of wine. I even thought, *Maybe the wine will help me stop shaking.* The anxiety was getting so bad that my jaw was starting to seize up, and I was having difficulty speaking. When the wine arrived, the glass was filled to the brim. I knew I couldn't pick it up without spilling it. My date lowered his head to write our order for lunch, and I quickly grabbed the glass with both hands and took a gulp.

In that moment, I believe, I became an alcoholic. It was like a switch was thrown in my head. I could feel the alcohol going through me. It was like a gift from the gods. It washed away all the anxiety immediately.

I was able to relax and enjoy the lunch. We had a very nice time and agreed to go to the birthday party the following Saturday.

Afterward, I went home and told my friends how I made a fool of myself on the date. All week I kept worrying about the next date and wondered if I would shake again. Just the thought of it made me shake again. Finally, a neighbor said to me, "Oh, for God's sake, have a drink before he gets there." Yes, that was the solution, I never would have thought of that; I never did anything like that before. And that's exactly what I did. I never went out with that man again without having a drink first. It was never a problem when I was with him because everything we did included alcohol. He was a big drinker.

The next year was the best of my life and the worst of my life. I knew this man was everything I had ever dreamed of. I also knew I wasn't ready for a relationship. My nerves were shot. I hadn't healed from my first marriage. I was using alcohol to feel and act normal. I didn't use it to get drunk, nor did I use it all the time. Everyone around me was saying how lucky I was. Many people envied me. No one, except for one close friend, knew how I was using liquor to medicate myself.

Within three months, he proposed to me. I told him that I knew I loved him and wanted to marry him, but that I just didn't know when. Nonetheless, he began looking for a house for us. I would have to take a few gulps of Scotch before going to meet the realtor and him. He took me to Bermuda in June while my two girls were away with their father. I was so anxious about going and flying (I still suffered from claustrophobia and couldn't stand being locked in the plane) that I drank and drank and drank. I had such an acute anxiety attack in a ladies' room in Bermuda that I begged some stranger to go get me a double scotch from the bar. She did. I was a mess. I was falling apart.

Already, just five months from the day we met, the alcohol had turned on me, but I desperately needed it. I didn't know what else to do. I didn't know what else to use other than alcohol. I finally told him that I was falling apart and that I needed some time. He and everyone else couldn't understand what my problem was, since it was obvious to everyone that he was the answer to my problems—no more watching other parents' kids, no more tenant, no more problems.

In September 1983, I went to the doctor and told him that I was drinking to stay calm. I told him that I knew it wasn't right or safe, and that I didn't want to do it. I also told him I needed help. He said, "Thank God you came before you became an alcoholic. I'll give you a drug to relieve your anxiety attacks and eliminate your need for alcohol." He gave me Xanax.

I took the Xanax as prescribed. It seemed to help a little. We were planning to get married December 5, 1983. A week or so before the wedding, the anxiety attacks started again. I didn't know what else to do except drink a glass of wine along with the Xanax. I was afraid to mix alcohol and drugs. I knew it was wrong, and I was afraid I was going to die if I did. I told the doctor at my next visit. He said that it wouldn't kill me, but that it wasn't a good idea to mix the two. Despite his warning, I continued to mix them to control my anxiety. The effect was devastating. I began to black out.

We moved into our new home on December 3 and got married December 5. I had my husband's company over in mid-December and forty relatives on Christmas Day. I felt I had to have everything set up, decorated, and wonderful. I felt I couldn't say "No." (Not only had I learned never to say no, I had never even thought to say no.)

In January 1984, we went to visit his parents in Florida. I was the new daughter-in-law. I was taking Xanax and drinking. I snuck out to buy liquor while I was there, even though the house was full of liquor. I passed out and slept through dinner one night. When I arrived home, I went into a blackout. My husband told me the only way he could calm me down was make love to me. I didn't remember making love. The next day my husband told me that Xanax was really bad for me. He's very much against drugs and didn't like me taking it. I stopped the Xanax cold turkey. I called the doctor and asked him if I could die if I just stopped taking the pills. He said, "No, but why torture yourself?"

I flushed the pills down the toilet. I later learned that I could have gone into convulsions and died from stopping abruptly. In fact, Xanax is highly addictive, and when I was taking it, it more than tripled my need for alcohol. I went through a week of withdrawal. It was terrifying. I had auditory hallucinations. I could clearly hear radio broadcasts even though the radio was turned off. I kept checking to make sure the radio wasn't on. By the end of the week, I could just put tiny pieces of food in my mouth because I didn't remember how to chew. My husband was supportive because he wanted me off the Xanax. My daughters went to school each day, and I told them I had a terrible flu. I remember thinking during that week that my goal was to be able to make a cup of tea. I was like an exposed, raw nerve. During the day, I kept the shades down because the light hurt my eyes.

Look at where I had gone in one year's time—from being on a nervous blind date to being a full-blown alcoholic. By St. Patrick's Day 1984, I was feeling and looking good again. Both my husband and I agreed that I could drink safely again now that I was rid of those awful pills. I did. I also terminated my visits to the psychiatrist. I realized that he was not helping me. I felt that the worst was over, that I just needed some time to adjust to my new life.

At the end of May 1984, we went on a belated honeymoon to France. It was wonderful, but I knew that when I drank it triggered more anxiety. I still drank a lot on planes. In July, we were doing a lot of entertaining, and I was feeling overwhelmed. But I felt I had to do it; I didn't want to blow my image or let my husband down. After a weekend of nonstop entertaining I spent Monday drinking. When my husband came home from work, I was drunk and crying. The next day I did the same. My sister happened to call me, and I was crying and carrying on over the phone. She was so upset that she came out to see me. You see, I had always been the one in control. Responsible, reliable, and capable. Even though I felt like I was falling apart and had a strong desire to run away (from what I'm not sure), no one else knew.

My sister was shocked when she saw me, so she called my mother. My mother came out the next day. She was shocked, too. She told me she thought I needed to go to a hospital. I said I would. I felt I desperately needed a rest and a good checkup. I called the local hospital's detox center. Even though it was a ten-day program, I told them I could only stay for five days because I had company coming. My husband and mother agreed. My husband's niece and nephew from Florida were supposed to come up for a visit. The counselor at the hospital agreed to my terms. I was up that entire night with agitation, even though I hadn't had a drink in over twenty-four hours. My husband brought me to the hospital the next day. We told everyone I had an ulcer. They all believed it because of all that had happened in the last year. I can remember sitting and waiting in the Emergency Room and praying that I wouldn't see anyone that I knew, and thinking how I couldn't believe my life had reached this low point. I have never felt such shame.

When the doctor told me that I was an alcoholic, I almost died. I knew that I had been using alcohol to medicate myself and had become dependent on it, but I never dreamed I was an alcoholic. I didn't know that it didn't matter how much I drank or for how long I drank, what mattered was what the drinking did to me. I felt terrified, alone, and hated myself for getting into this predicament. Even though they explained to me that alcoholism is a disease, I still felt ashamed, embarrassed, and responsible.

When I told my mother and husband that I was an alcoholic, they both said, "That's crazy, you hardly drank. What about your anxiety?" The doctor said, "Well, then you've got two problems—alcoholism and anxiety." I knew that I had to stay the full ten days. I did. The other clients laughed at my drinking history. They told me that I was crazy to be there. The counselor didn't recommend further treatment for me. (To tell you the truth, I think they thought I'd be back.) I went home ten days later. The doctor and the counselor said their main concern for me was my husband's drinking.

My husband picked me up from the hospital. We had only been married eight months. I was scared. I had never been without alcohol in our relationship. We had a quiet day and my husband said he would clear our social calendar for one month. He had a drink within the first hour I was home.

I was told to go to ninety AA meetings in ninety days and attend a weekly after-care session. I did. I was afraid to drink. Living sober was so scary for me because I still had all the anxieties and didn't know how to deal with them. Even though I was terrified to go to AA, I sensed there was something in those rooms that I had always wanted but never had. Regardless of what I was feeling, I kept going to meetings. I was too afraid to speak and would get very nervous. But I heard that the healing was in the sharing, so I found smaller meetings where I felt more comfortable. To this day I don't share at huge meetings, I still get too anxious.

I've heard many people say that when they came to AA the weight of the world lifted off their shoulders. I felt like a huge weight was put on my shoulders. It felt like a big, heavy responsibility I had to carry for the rest of my life.

Four months later, I was still attending daily AA meetings. I had met people I trusted and liked, and I enjoyed the meetings. I was still attending after-care, too.

My husband's company was having a ground-breaking ceremony that I was supposed to attend. Fifteen minutes before I had to leave the house, I began shaking. It was an attack like I had on our first date. I had no desire to drink, but I didn't know how else to stop the shaking. I poured some vodka and drank it. I drank a couple more shots in the bathroom when I got to the event. The shakes stopped. I was fine for the ceremony.

But I wasn't really fine. I was still troubled. I had not yet learned how to take care of myself. I had not yet learned that I didn't have to go to the ground-breaking ceremony. I was still living my life on the premise that it's more important what other people think of me than what I think of myself. Later that day, I told my husband, my after-care group, and my AA meeting that I drank. I continued to go to AA.

On our first wedding anniversary, my husband and I went to a romantic country inn for dinner. He drank throughout the evening. After dinner I had a sip of his brandy. On January 5, 1985, we attended an annual black-tie affair in New York City. Each year my husband's partners and company attorney attend. We planned to spend Saturday and Sunday in the city. While getting dressed for the dinner, I began to shake. I called my AA sponsor in New Jersey. Just speaking to her calmed me down. My husband also said, "We won't go until you feel ready." This helped me a lot. I got through the evening sober. Out of the ten people at our table, I was the only one not drinking. My mistake was not going home afterward, but staying and meeting the same people the next day for brunch. Everyone was drinking champagne. At brunch, when asked what I would like, I said, "Oh, I don't know . . . " and my husband said, "A little white wine should be okay." I said, "Okay." I desperately wanted to be a part of the group. I felt so different and alone. I shouldn't have been there. It was too much for me to handle. I had one glass of wine. I felt the effects. I didn't like it. I had become used to being in control of my mind. I told my husband on the way home that I didn't like the way the wine made me feel. I thought of how I liked my AA friends better.

That was my last drink: January 6, 1985.

My first year of sobriety was probably the hardest year of my life. I didn't change anything, except that I didn't drink and I went to lots of AA meetings. It was the fear of what drinking could do to me that kept me in AA the first few years, not a love of sobriety. I came to learn that rather than cure anxiety, alcohol only creates more agitation. For every hour of sedation, there's a paycheck of three hours of agitation. In other words, alcohol just wouldn't work anymore for me. What terrified me was how quickly alcoholism progressed within my body. I knew that my tolerance for alcohol was gone. I believed the experts when they told me it's a chronic, progressive, and fatal disease. And most importantly, I knew that when I drank it made me feel insane. I couldn't do that to my daughters and husband. I couldn't bear the pain and shame it would bring them. I also knew how hard it was when I first got sober, and I couldn't stand the thought of having to go through that again.

My greatest challenge has been to face my fears. I would say that my main reason for coming into AA was to overcome fear and to learn to live comfortably in my own skin. I knew that liquor didn't work anymore. I knew that alcohol only magnified and multiplied my fears. Drinking filled me with irrational fear. I didn't know where it came from; I only knew that it gripped my insides and paralyzed me. It made me afraid to answer the phone, afraid to go to the store, afraid to tell anyone how I felt.

I believe there is a power in AA that is greater than this fear. My husband and I went to a dinner-dance early in my sobriety. When I started to dance for the first time sober, I began to shake. I stopped and walked outside to the parking lot. I thought I would try walking the anxiety away. I kept walking and walking around the parking lot, saying, "If you want me sober then you had better help me." I'm not sure who I was talking to; I think I was reaching out to any power out there in the universe who would help me.

My husband was with me, he was drinking, and kept saying, "I don't deserve this. I didn't get married for this to happen." After a few minutes, I felt better and was able not only to go back inside, but to dance every dance for the rest of the night. At that point my husband was drunk and saying to me, "Oh, I think you're so wonderful. I love you so much." For the first time I realized that I was going to have to take care of myself, but AA and a power greater than myself would be there to help me.

I've had many experiences where my fear rises up and grabs me, but I've never been deluded again into thinking alcohol is the answer. I know it is not.

Nine months after I entered the program, my best friend died of the same kind of cancer my sister died of. She was the friend who watched my children for me when I went into detox, the only friend who knew that I was in AA. When she was in the hospital, I was afraid to go and see her, but I knew I had to. I remember driving to the hospital and repeating the Serenity Prayer over and over out loud. When I got to the hospital, I started to shake. My claustrophobia was so bad that I took the stairs to the fourth floor because I couldn't take the elevator. When I walked into her room, she had severe tremors from the medication the doctor had given her. She didn't even notice that I was shaking, too. I sat down and talked to her. That night I went back to the hospital. Her husband was there, too. I knew she was dying, and I called her mother and told her to come. A strength and calm was with me that I had never known before. We were with her when she died. I was very sad, but I had no regrets. The next day I went to my usual Tuesday AA meeting and just sat in the back of the room and cried. I knew that was where I needed to be. As painful as it was, I knew the greatest tribute I could pay to my friend would be to stay sober. I grieved her death, my loss, but I didn't need a drink. I felt the feelings and shared them with AA.

Two years after my introduction to AA, I went back to college. One of my dreams was to finish my education. As scary as it was, I just kept going, one course at a time. I graduated in 1995.

I quit smoking when I was in AA almost three years. What's the point of working so hard to live sober if I just die of lung cancer? I couldn't stand that thought. So I went to a hypnotist. I haven't had a cigarette in more than eight years. I've wanted a cigarette many times and still miss it now and then, but I won't smoke because I know that one will lead me right back.

When I was in the program a year, I helped run a women's AA meeting at a local rehabilitation facility for indigent women. I loved it. All my life I felt I wanted to do something worthwhile, something with meaning, something that might make even a little difference. I found that something at this rehab. I slowly began learning and volunteering time. I went to school for four years and became a certified alcohol counselor five years ago. I still volunteer at the rehab, and I've become a member of their Board of Trustees. I've found my passion.

When I was sober five years, I sat down with my

daughters and told them that I was an alcoholic and that I was in AA. They knew I went to school for alcoholism and that I helped women alcoholics, but they didn't know the whole truth. Because my drinking was brief and I was not drunk around them, they had no idea that I was an alcoholic. For five years I carried shame and a fear that they would think less of me as a mother. I couldn't bear that. They had always been so precious to me. I finally became uncomfortable with the fact that they didn't know the truth. I had built it up in my head that they would react badly. But when I told them, they said they never remembered me drinking, and then asked whether that was all I wanted to tell them. They had thought it was going to be something more exciting because I had made special tea.

When I was seven years sober, my younger daughter was diagnosed with a very serious disease. She required extensive testing and a fifteen-day hospital stay for major surgery. She continues to be monitored and takes daily medication. It was the most difficult and frightening experience of my life. I credit my Higher Power and AA for giving me the courage and the wisdom to go through that ordeal. I have no regrets in the way I handled any of it. So much growth and positive energy came out of such a dark experience. My daughters and I are closer than we ever were. My husband and I are closer. Our family unit is closer and stronger.

My older daughter went off to college. I'm here to love, support, and encourage her. She's always had a tough time in school, but I never gave up on her. I need to constantly be willing to change, keep an open mind, and, perhaps, learn a better way.

My husband and I celebrated our twelfth anniversary in December 1995. He still drinks. Alcohol is still a very important part of his life. I believe that the powerful force that attracted us at the beginning continues to bond our souls. We have grown and stretched beyond our wildest imaginations. We have surmounted difficulties that we would have thought impossible. It has not been easy. Our lives have taken a path we probably would never have chosen, but I believe it has made us stronger, wiser and more tolerant people. I love him very much.

I continue to go to the same meetings that I started out at eleven years ago. My life is full. I belong to several women's groups. I bounce my thoughts and feelings off a therapist once a month. She has been like a mentor to me. I continue to actively work on my sobriety one day at a time, realizing that it is process, a slow process.

I continue to learn who I am and how to care for and love that person. Spirituality is the essence of my program. My two favorite prayers are "Help Me" and "Thank You." I'm grateful to God for answering my cry for help in the way He saw most fit. I need to know that there is a much larger picture than just the tiny piece I'm able to see. I feel the greatest gift I have gotten from AA is courage. I define courage as being afraid and doing it anyway. AA is a program of action, and I'm gradually becoming the woman I've always wanted to be. Isn't it interesting that what I thought was the lowest point of my life was actually the beginning of the life I had always wanted. I just needed to be willing to do my part. The rest would be taken care of. I pray every day for continued willingness.

Rhoda's Story

I grew up in an upper-middle class family. My father was a lawyer who played the violin in symphony orchestras. My mother was a college graduate with a mind hungry for ideas, philosophies, and social ideologies. We worshiped at the altar of culture and intellect. But despite our sophistication and wisdom, excruciating unhappiness permeated our home. The members of my family seemed to be directly responsible for each other's unhappiness. The two most popular phrases in our house were: "Look what you made me do," and "I can't stand it."

My father, Meyer, expressed his rage and pain by yelling and chain-smoking. Frances, my mother, expressed her unhappiness by taking to her bed in a "nervous breakdown" after her father died when I was four years old. My older sister dealt with her anger by yelling, cursing, or lying face down, motionless in her bed. My grandmother controlled all of us by screaming and making us feel guilty when she did not get her way.

My father's addiction to nicotine seemed harmless when compared with the self-destructive habits of the rest of the family. We found refuge in food, stuffing our despair. To make matters worse, our daily routine included little physical activity—locking in all of the negatives with no way of discharging the energy. I, however, sought refuge in dance. Dancing helped me deal with my pent-up anger and inner confusion that twisted my stomach into pretzel-like knots. Each night I would dance to the music of the famous Russian composers, transforming myself from an overweight matzo ball into a sensuous Isadora Duncan.

Because my mother had largely abdicated her parenting role, my relationship with my father was obsessively strong. Although I was terrified of his hot temper, I loved him fiercely. I was his beloved, his favorite object. I got good grades, played the violin and piano, and was inordinately precocious. I continually tried to please Daddy, to delight Daddy, to help Daddy overcome his pain caused by the emotional deprivation that he was experiencing with my mother and sister. I would win Daddy's love anew every day, knowing how desperately he needed my achievements. And how much I needed his love.

My emotional attachment to my father was still strong as I entered college. He drove me up to Brandeis University at the start of my freshman year. Before driving off he said, "This is the fulfillment of my dreams." Two weeks later he was dead of a heart attack. The Jewish-American princess with a brilliant future was undone, destroyed, horrified, shocked beyond any nightmare. I was stuck in a never-ending inner screaming, and locked in angst. The journey into the dark underworld had officially begun. The first part of the journey, however, was not without love and excitement for the universe. My "higher power" placed in my life an abundance of friends who shared from the soul, and experiences that introduced me to a wild genius inside of me, a wildness and creativity that I would come to love and trust as intrinsic to my nature. The drug of choice at that time was food. Lots of food and lots of sweets. There were no other mind-altering drugs or alcohol at that time.

Then the darkest, most destructive aspect of this voyage ensued. It was as if evil itself came to claim me. At the end of my junior year at Brandeis, I was totally exhausted, so my mother took me to see a doctor. The doctor was obese. He also had a habit of prescribing thyroid pills to everyone who was "overweight." I weighed about 123 pounds, which was only eight or nine pounds over my ideal weight. Nonetheless, I was given a prescription for three grams of thyroid a day, a dose normally prescribed for people who have their thyroid glands removed. For the first time since my father's death, I had energy. I was speeding without knowing it. I loved it. I did more, lost lots of weight, and was always in a state of high excitation. I also slept less and less. Near the end of my first semester of my senior year, while on full scholarship and going for Magna Cum Laude and Phi Beta Kappa (a very important part of my identity), I stopped sleeping altogether. I began to shake all over and felt tremors racing through my body. Nothing I tried would make it go away. The symptoms continued unabated until my mother flew up to school. She offered me a glass of wine to help me relax. I needed to drink the whole bottle to relax. At that scurrilous moment, I became an alcoholic and mentally ill.

I took a leave of absence from college, returned to a broken family, and was "treated" by psychiatry with tranquilizers and anti-depressants, all liberally mixed with large quantities of alcohol. Alcohol and drugs accompanied me everywhere: to teaching jobs after I finally graduated from college; to graduate school; to the local community college where I taught for four years; to concerts; through relationships.

The year was 1977. I was chemically insane without ever realizing that I was suffering from a disease called alcoholism and drug addiction. I was relying on that inner core of intellect, creativity, and music—which by then was completely polluted by this disease—when I arrived at the Fair Oaks Alcoholic Unit in Summit, New Jersey. To my shock and horror, I was forced to confront Rhoda, the drug-addicted alcoholic who had caused her own brain damage. No one seemed to understand that all I had was my educated brain, and that I had, volitionally, or so it seemed, destroyed it. Of course, in this horrific predicament, I could not understand that I could get well, could heal, or even deserved to live. I could not, and would not, understand this new language that was being offered to me. Surrender to what? A higher power? My higher power was music—my ability to sing, to teach, to create. I had ruined that, so it followed logically that suicide was the only rational option.

My condition deteriorated into a hideous state, an inner hell. I experienced a tormented metamorphosis. I became an expressionless, insomniac zombie, lacking all save a lifeless carcass with the fires of hell burning inside. I felt numb, tortured, dead. Deprived of the most basic animal senses, I no longer could taste, smell, see clearly, or cry. I didn't even receive internal messages to the brain telling me that I needed to go to the bathroom. I was dead, but I could not die. I was in hell with no grace, no relief. So this is what they meant by eternal damnation. I had learned the doctrine well, even though I had never had any formal religious training.

There were several unsuccessful suicide attempts during this tortured zombie syndrome. There were also several unsuccessful attempts at AA. After Fair Oaks, I had no doubts that I was an alcoholic. But AA was not for me. My early AA experiences left me untouched, even repulsed. I could not identify with the people, the "drunk-a-logs," the slogans. What I felt was a lack of sensibility, awareness, and acculturation. It would be many years before I could experience the wisdom, depth, and power of AA. Basically an outsider in mainstream society, I continued this pattern in AA.

In 1977, I stopped drinking alcohol, and taking prescription drugs except for some anti-depressants when the syndrome would seize me. In 1978, my mother—who had taken me to the thyroid doctor and given me the first alcoholic drink—introduced me to Unity of Montclair, where I was to experience my initial recovery, create a healing consciousness, and embrace my new identity as a spiritual being. I was guided through the "higher worlds" of metaphysics, healing, and consciousness by an inspired woman, a Unity minister. The minister helped me to see a greater purpose for all the suffering, suffused me with her own enlightened soul, and taught me to look for the deeper spiritual meaning in all events in the outer world. She taught me that my words and thoughts were creative, that I could create and recreate my world through creating thoughts and words with awareness, that I could experience the sacred realm of divine consciousness through disciplined prayer and meditation. I learned that I, as a spiritual being and "Child of God," was automatically forgiven, and was beginning to experience grace. This soft, loving, highly aesthetic approach to healing was roughly juxtaposed to the AA way. It was a world away from the one AA sponsor who continually judged and criticized me, and attempted to control me through insult and threat by repeatedly telling me I was a "lying-in-the-gutter drunk" and a "congenital defective." I left AA without looking back, and stayed close to Unity. I also entered the world of holistic health when I became the patient of a New Age chiropractor who was purported to be a psychic healer, nutritionist, genius, and all-around phenomenon.

Relapse

In 1980, I had a relapse. The cause an uncontrollable rage toward a woman in whose house I was living. I became a patient of the "miraculous one." And what of alcohol and drugs? What of the deep wound and soul sickness of the disease? It was totally denied by me and by those around me. In Unity, I was forever in light. All the rest was dismissed. There could be no authentic recovery as there was no acknowledgment. My mother continued to assert that how I was behaving just "wasn't me." The doctor continued to state emphatically that I had no "alcoholic vibes." He even prescribed several glasses of wine each week as part of my new "holistic health" regimen. I had known better for several years, but then began to forget. My alcoholism was growing wild in the dark waters of denial, jammed down deep in my unconscious.

I wasn't aware that my disease was getting progressively worse. My addiction transferred from alcohol to the doctor, and he encouraged my addiction to him, exploiting me physically, emotionally, psychically, sexually, and spiritually. He became my "higher power," my salvation, my guru, my betrayer, eventually creating the seeds for my relapse and return to AA. A few years earlier, I would allow myself an occasional glass of wine, rationalizing the indiscretion by foolishly believing that I had no "alcoholic vibes." The drinking binges became more frequent. Then a big crisis hit. The good doctor started having sex with me in his office and told me that he loved me. It was a short-lived romance. The doctor abruptly informed me that he was getting engaged to his secretary. I left him, against his will, in despair and rage. I got drunk several times and experienced a complete emotional breakdown, a severe psychic dismemberment from which I was convinced I would never recover.

The year was 1989. Despite the insanity of those "doctor-addicted" years, I accomplished some amazing things. Flying on the wings of psychic addiction, I created courses, concerts, music and healing seminars at the New School for Social Research, New York University, and at holistic centers. My skills and talents expanded, along with the dark disease that grew silently and deadly, until it finally destroyed me. The agitated zombie took over again. This time there was no doubt what had created it. I was completely disabled and was forced to seek relief again from anti-depressants. This went on for years.

Finally, I returned to AA. This time I was mature enough to listen, learn, grow, and share my experiences with others. I gained a deep respect for the wisdom of the program. With the help of other AA members, I learned how to forgive myself for past mistakes and examined the true nature of my addiction. In short, I began to realize what a huge impact drinking was having on my life.

The year was 1994. I was growing, changing and had a stronger relationship with my "inner power." I accepted that I was an alcoholic, with a disease that requires vigilance, care, and attention. I recognized that I had a strong spiritual consciousness that needed devotion and dedication. I was self-supporting, thanks to my talent, training, and education. I'd also learned to use the experience of my illness to assist, educate, and support healing in my clients and students.

How It Is Now

The most difficult task of all is to describe, and be

explicit about, the now, the present. Drugs and alcohol are no longer an active part of my consciousness, and yet aspects of the "ism" hang on to me. Resentment and blame cling to me like a needy child. Procrastination and lethargy accompany me during the empty hours. Pregnant with creative potential, the alcoholic Rhoda will look for something else to eat, sit in a purposeless stupor, obediently lobotomized in front of the greatest religion of the twentieth century—the television. My creativity cries out for me to be with it, to use, practice, express my sacred gifts, but I snuff its need. My life in the "outer" world is created exclusively by my consciousness, education, training, and talent. I work as a hypnotist and holistic counselor, working with groups and giving seminars. I go back, almost daily now, to my original ecstasy: singing and music. This is a blessing to me, and my work continually expresses this "essence of self," apparently untouched by dark personal history and depression. Singing is the vehicle by which I express those qualities that I both love and need. Things such as warmth, insight, intuition, enthusiasm, and excitement. When I create the space for song, when I let go and surrender to it, the music creates itself through me, always giving me more than I give it, creating and recreating a strange and powerful identity, a mystical sense of "for this I was born."

I am struggling with the enormous detour of my alcoholism and mental illness, which remains seemingly haphazard and destructive. I have yet to say that I can fully see the wisdom and purpose for all of those tortured and lost years, and yet I was asked to facilitate a "women in recovery" group, from which this writing is derived. In these psycho-spiritual sessions, I began to get a glimmer of their wisdom and purpose, a sense of timelessness and connection to the women and spirit that could not have existed without the "non-being" of the alcoholic experience.

I totally espouse the idea that everything I need is within me. At this time, the enormous challenge is to access it, use it, live it. Frances, my mother, who is approaching the age of eighty-six, has cancer. I, her daughter, am a very reluctant caretaker, shopper, chauffeur, errand runner. Facing all of my issues—fear, illness, death, unresolved anger, and resentment, stemming from early childhood to the present—my intention is to move through these experiences with awareness, with mindfulness, with my "inner power." My prayer is to make peace with my past, with Frances, with death and dying.

I have been working with women and female spirituality for several years—psychology, mythology, "goddess" work. I believe that I carry the grief and the beauty of my "sisters" in my heart. I feel honored and "chosen" to do this work.

. . . And so it is.

Bridget's Story

I drank beer, smoked pot, and popped pills. I sniffed heroin, too. But my downfall was cocaine.

Smoking coke brought me to my knees. I spent most of my life running after cocaine. I beat people for it. I stole from my brother and lied to my mother. I even sold my body for it. I risked my life hopping into cars with strange men in an attempt to separate them from their wallets. I stayed up until all hours of the night and sometimes didn't come home for two or three days. When I did make it home, my lips would be as white as snow and my stomach would be growling from lack of food.

I wasn't always a drug addict. Once, I was just a kid. I was the second child born to a mother who did drugs and a father who didn't stay around long enough to raise me. When I was twelve, my mother told me and my brother that she did drugs. (I guess she was trying to forget her troubles.) After she and my father split up, she married my baby brother's father. My stepfather used to beat her up real bad. My brother and I used to sit our room sometimes and listen to my mother scream. But there was nothing we could do.

Despite everything, my mom was a caring and loving person. It was just hard for her to show us how much she loved us. The love I did receive came from my grandmother, a dear friend who meant the world to me. She was everything I could hope for in a person. Grandparents always have a favorite grandchild, and I was Grandma's favorite. But then Grandma got real sick. She had gangrene and had to get her toes amputated. It got worse, and she had to get her leg amputated. Grandma's illness took everything away from me. I didn't have anyone to lean on or to talk to.

My grandmother's situation upset me so much that I just stopped caring. I didn't want to talk to anybody. I hated myself. I thought that if I got in trouble, people would leave me alone. I started getting suspended from school so that I could stay home and take care of my grandmother. She always used to take care of me when I was a kid. If I caught a cold, she would stay up late at night making me chicken noodle soup so that when I woke up I could have a nice bowl of hot soup sitting there waiting for me. That's why I love her so much. When my grandmother first got sick, I wasn't taking drugs. I was just angry about her being ill and started getting wild.

I started getting into trouble at school. The teachers wanted to put me in a special education class because they said I couldn't adjust to a regular, normal class with all the other kids. They put me in a class with about eight students where I could get special attention. My teacher, Ms. Poole, wouldn't take any of my crap. I was classified as this tough, bad girl, but Ms. Poole didn't pay any attention. She cared about me and worked with me. Still, I went from one special ed class to another because of my bad attitude. The teachers didn't like my disposition and couldn't deal with the way I talked to them. I ran into another teacher, Mrs. Jefferson, who broke me in real hard, too. Without their help, I would never have stayed in school. I wound up going to Elizabeth High School in tenth grade. I fought every day. I fought and fought. The Board of Education kicked me out of school and I transferred to St. Anthony's Catholic school in Newark, New Jersey, run by nuns. The nuns took an interest in me. I couldn't figure out why. Sister Pat and Sister Ann helped me in school. I did so well that I was able to transfer back to Elizabeth High, where I graduated. My grandmother always told me, "Bridget, if you don't do nothing else in life, graduate high school." I did.

My grandmother's illness got progressively worse. She lost her other leg. I didn't handle it very well. I was still getting into lots of trouble and throwing my little scenes. I popped anyone who got in my way. One day, my grandmother asked my mother to bring me to see her so she could talk to me. She said, "Bridget, you know I love you, but I want you to know this before anybody else: I can't hold on no more!" A week later my mother's sister called. I knew something was wrong. So I asked her if anything was wrong with Grandma. She wouldn't answer. She said she wanted to speak to my mom. Then my mom screamed, "Grandma's dead." She was gone.

That was the worst day of my life. I felt like a part of me was gone.

After Grandma's death. I started to smoke pot with my cousins. I started drinking, too. I was eighteen. We used to get little bags of weed, roll up joints, and sit around laughing and giggling about how it was okay to be poor. Then I moved on to other drugs. I took codeine. I took pills. I liked the feeling; it took me somewhere else I wanted to be. I didn't want to deal with the fact that my grandmother was dead.

Then I moved on to sniffing heroin. I was with my cousin the first time I did a bag of heroin. But he wasn't the only family member I partied with. I used to get high with my mother and brother, too. I used to think it was cool because I thought the best people to get high with was your family. I didn't know any better.

I started doing cocaine when I was twenty. Cocaine was the worst drug of all: To get it, you have to chase it. One hit was never enough. My cousin and I used to stay out all night smoking that stuff. Cocaine stripped me of everything.

I didn't care what it took to get the next hit. I used to take soap, crush it up, put it in a vial, and go over to my dealer's house. When I got the chance, I'd switch the stuff up. Sometimes I'd get caught and end up in a fight. If I was really hard up for cash, I would let guys pick me up in their cars and make them think I was going to have sex with them. After they got their clothes off, I'd get them all riled up, take their wallets without them knowing, and then tell them that I wasn't doing nothing to them. Then I'd jump out of the car and run.

My craving for drugs was so intense I even stole from my brother. He was a dealer, and I used to steal drugs from him. He didn't know it, though, because he was usually too high to keep track of his stash. One of my worst experiences was when my brother and I got into an argument because he wouldn't share a bag of heroin with me. We ended up fighting. We argued, hit each other, and then I got so angry that I got a bat and hit him in the head. My brother had to get stitches in his head. That was one of my biggest mistakes because my brother is my pride and joy. We experience a lot of stuff together. We even got our tonsils out at the same time. I love my brother. And if my mother didn't do anything else, she taught us that we are all we have and that we should never let anyone come between us.

When we first moved to the projects in 1977, I used to go around and clean old peoples' houses. When my addiction got worse and I needed cash, I used to steal money from their homes. It was easy because they knew me and didn't think I'd rob them. I used to go to one old lady's house, do my cleaning, and then rip her off. I never used violence or put my hands on her. One day after robbing her, I went back to her house and saw her on the floor. I thought to myself, *Good, I'm not the only one coming up here taking her money.* I figured she had hit her face on the table. I got her up and called 911. Then I left. I went back the next day because I knew it was Social Security check day. She let me in and five minutes later the police showed up. One of the cops told me to stand in the hallway. The other officer talked to the woman and then told me they wanted to lock me up. I told the officer to call my mom. They showed up at her place with a search warrant, raided her house, and locked her up, too. When we got down to the police station, they took my mother in first and questioned her. She was all uptight. When she came downstairs to see me, she said, "Baby, I don't know what's going on, but cooperate with these police. Just get Mommy out of here."

And I said, "Okay, Mom." Then they took me up to a room. I knew I could get my mother out of there if I signed the papers. Not knowing any better, I signed the papers and wound up "admitting" that I hit the lady and took her money. They said I was gonna do ten to twenty years.

I wound up going to jail. They wanted me to plead guilty, but I wouldn't. I told them I wanted to take it to trial. They kept me in the county jail for a year awaiting trial. They kept telling my mother to talk to me, to get me to plead guilty. I said, "Mom, I'm not guilty." Like I said, I would have pleaded guilty to taking the money, but as far as doing bodily harm, I wasn't going to do it. No way. The day I went to court, I was ready to go to trial.

My lawyer came to me and said, "Bridget, listen. This is gonna be tough. They are going to bring this old lady in on a stretcher, and when they see her and they see you, you're going to be in trouble." I got scared. I didn't know what to do because I was dealing with a public defender.

They took me to the rear chamber, and one of my brother's friends was there to help me. He said, "Bridget, I'm not trying to tell you what to do, but the way I see it, they are trying to get you and I would suggest you take the plea." The plea was eight years flat. I asked to see my mother and told her that I wasn't lying to her, that I didn't beat up the old lady like they were saying.

My mother said, "Baby, you gotta do what you gotta do." I wound up taking the plea. I got locked up October 5, 1980.

I was scared when I got to prison. I didn't know what to expect, I thought to myself, *Lord, what did I get myself into.* I saw all kinds of women there: women who had molested their children; a woman who killed somebody because their brother had sex with a whore. I didn't let anybody get close to me. I didn't talk to nobody. I wasn't gonna be staying with nobody. I saw all these gay women, all messing with each other, and talking and feeling. And I thought to myself, *Damn, I'm supposed to be here to get help.* Whatever. I did what I was supposed to do. I didn't make any friends. I just did what I had to do.

When I got out of jail in 1991, all I had on my mind was having a beer. So I did. I figured that was better than buying a bag of dope. Then I started smoking cocaine again. I sneaked it and nobody knew. A lot of my friends sold drugs and, thinking I was straight, let me hold their packages for them. I did their coke. I kept getting high until my parole officer made me take a urine test. My urine was dirty. They told me I had to go to an outpatient clinic.

I remember taking another urine test and still getting high. They sent me back to the county jail, where I stayed for fourteen days. After being released, I was back out there getting high again. Sniffing that dope, smoking that coke. I was way out there. I was doing it all.

Then it happened again: I failed another urine test. My parole officer told me that they wouldn't arrest me if I put myself in a detox and stayed there. I signed myself into the detox at St. Elizabeth Hospital. The detox was for seven days. I couldn't stay for seven days. I wound up getting arrested and was sent back to the county jail. I wrote to Trenton and told them that I wasn't a criminal, that I was back in jail because I have a drug problem. I asked them to send me somewhere to get help. Sending me back to prison wasn't going to help me. They kept me locked up anyway. Finally, someone from Trenton came to see me. She took down some information and asked me if I would like to go to a drug rehabilitation program in Atlantic City, New Jersey. I said yes. She told me they would get back to me. But before I made it into the program, they sent me back to prison for twelve more months. I was devastated. I was hurt. I didn't know what to do. I made up my mind to do it right this time. I knew that I was not gonna go back there ever again. I was tired, really tired.

When my twelve months were almost up, they called me to the main building to talk to me. They told me I was recommended to go to Turning Point, a rehab in Verona, New Jersey, and that I had to let them know in a few hours. With attitude I said, "I'm not going to no Turning Point." I called my family for advice, and they told me to try it. "Whatever," I said. To myself I said, *Bridget, you've never been in a program. You might as well go ahead and go for it. Try it.* I was scared, but I ended up going to Turning Point.

The second week at Turning Point, Jane, one of the counselors, got fed up with my attitude and told me that if I didn't like the way things were run there, to get out and go back to prison. Then I met another counselor, Susan. I don't know why, but Susan must have felt something for me. She wanted to help me. She made me sit down with my mother and express to her the way I was feeling, to be honest with her, and tell her how her addiction was hurting me. Once I was able to release that, I was able to face a lot more things. I never told people that my mother got high; I always kept it to myself because I didn't think it was anyone's business. In our house, what goes on in the house stays in the house.

That session with my mother put me on the road to recovery. I started accepting different things. Realizing that I wasn't by myself, I became more open-minded and started taking suggestions and stuff like that.

Before I got to Turning Point, I used to think drinking beer was okay. They made me see that alcohol is not okay, that it is the number one drug of them all. Turning Point helped me right from the start. I learned a lot. It's been more than three years since I last used drugs. My mother, though, still uses. It's her choice. It bothers me sometimes because I hate to see her the way she is. But she's still my mother, and I love her no matter what.

But me, I just can't get high no more. I realize that I can't pay somebody else's mortgage or car note; when you use and buy drugs, you just make somebody else rich. It's tough out on the streets, being sick and asking people for help. It's not like it used to be when we used to all put in $7.50 each, get a bag of dope, and think everything would be all right. Nowadays, you know, people die. What really made me come to my senses while I was at Turning Point was a letter a friend wrote me. She told me about this girl, Kit, who lived near me. The first time Kit smoked a bag of dope it turned out to be rat poison. She died. Kit was sixteen. I think that was my lowest point as a heroin addict. It could have been me. I still have that letter. I go back and read it when I get the urge to use drugs.

At Turning Point, I finally learned that I can live without alcohol and drugs. It's been almost four years since I had a drink or snorted heroin. I'm married. I work two jobs. I have a checking and savings account. I even have my own car.

My friends say I've changed a lot. They are proud of me and tell me I'm not the same old Bridget who used to hang out on street corners, getting high, fighting, arguing, and looking like a mess. When we get together, they say, "Bridget, you remember how you used to be. You used to sniff that dope and not care who you were with. Remember those days?" They keep my memory green, too. When I get too sassy, they let me know it: "Girl, don't forget where you came from." I appreciate that.

I'm sober today. It's been hard, but I like the change. I like not having to depend on chemical substances to get me up in the morning, to motivate me, to get me through the day. I don't have to pay anybody else's car payment or mortgage anymore. I have a choice today.

Jean's Story

She was Daddy's girl. Tall and slender, she wore clothes well, especially the cute dresses and tops Daddy picked out and bought for her as a reward for getting straight A's in school and being ranked first in her class. Her jewelry included a Phi Beta Kappa key and a gold medal in recognition of her academic proficiency in American Colonial History. She measured her words and spoke in soft tones. She was never guilty of raucous behavior. On the surface she appeared to be an exemplary young woman with a bright future. But beneath the exterior facade, all was not well. She was an alcoholic. She was a perfectionist with a desperate need, a craving really, to be in total control at all times. She had an overwhelming desire to please others. In the end, it was the terror of not being able to achieve true perfection that led to her drinking.

The above passage is a description of my personality on the eve of recognizing my addiction to alcohol. It marks the beginning of my personal journey to recovery with the help of Alcoholics Anonymous. Today, I understand that young woman much better. As a result, I am working hard on overcoming my character defects. I chart my course on the road to sobriety with the compass of moderation, not perfection. I now understand that I can make mistakes—or even fail—and still be a good person, perhaps even a better person for the lessons learned from my errors. I am no longer afraid to speak out and laugh at myself. I can recognize a down-to-earth side of my personality I never knew existed. Many good aspects of my personality that I foolishly ignored in the past have emerged. I got out of Jean's head and learned that I need other people, those who dislike me as well as those who do like me. Through the grace of God and the loving actions of my brother, Tom, I found AA twenty-five years ago.

I grew up a child of entitlement. My father was a physician who raised his family in a mansion with servants and indulged their every whim. As one of five children, I was accustomed to the best. I unconsciously accepted my father's belief that excellence always prevailed in his home, whether it be the house furnishings, the food served, the clothes worn, or the ideas that circulated in conversation, especially around the dinner table. We always had dinner at five o'clock so my father could preside over the family's affairs before he went to his evening office hours. At dinner, each child would describe his or her activities during the day. Daddy, however, would have the final word, and interpret the day's events for us through his eyes.

When I was a senior in college, my father decided that his three girls and two boys would learn about alcohol at home, not at a bar or at a wild fraternity party. Because of an intestinal problem, my father had a low tolerance for alcohol. He would sometimes take a glass of sherry in the winter or a light beer in the summer. Whether it was wine, beer, or hard liquor, he always served the best—and it was usually the strongest. Consequently, my tolerance for alcohol was very high. I could have a cocktail mixed with the highest proof alcohol before dinner, red or white wine with the main course, and a strong cordial afterward and never bat an eyelash. Believe it or not, I have only sat at a bar about three times in my entire life.

To all outward appearances, alcohol did not affect me adversely. But inside, where it really mattered, the effects were devastating. Whatever chance I had to recognize or correct my character defects—perfectionism and dependence—simply escaped me. I repeatedly made the wrong decisions, but was still supported by an indulgent father.

I graduated from college in 1941. But instead of going on to graduate school for a master's degree and then a doctorate in American History (history was my favorite subject in school, and I loved to do research), I chose to go to law school. I knew the first week of classes that it wasn't for me, but I didn't withdraw and register in the graduate history program, even though I wouldn't have lost any tuition money or missed any history classes. I finally left law school (without taking the final exams or receiving any credit for the semester's work) after Japan bombed Pearl Harbor.

I stumbled around from 1942 until my parents' deaths in 1960. It was kind of a "lost generation" for me. I bounced around in various jobs on Wall Street until the end of the World War II. Then I spent two years studying for a master's degree in American History. Although my sisters and most of my friends got married during the war, I did not. I dated a number of young men, as I had in college, but the one I wanted to marry was killed in 1944 during the war on a submarine in the Pacific Ocean. During the '50s I pursued a Ph.D. in History. I took all the required courses, picked a suitable dissertation topic and a mentor, and did all the long, tedious hours of research. I also took care of my elderly parents who were dying of heart disease. I worked as an adjunct professor at a nearby college, too. I had to explain constantly to my doctoral mentor that the care of my parents was delaying completion of my dissertation. He understood. But unfortunately for me, my drinking got worse. I relied on alcohol more and more to help deal with my frustration and the stress brought on by my parents' poor health. I believe I was a full-blown alcoholic by the time my father died early in 1960.

The shock of his death and the provisions of his will and that of my mother's, who died ten months later, made 1960 the worst year of my life. Because I was his favorite and had not married, my father was concerned about my future. He once told me that I needed the Ph.D. In order to get a decent-paying job. To everyone's surprise, his will stipulated that there was to be no distribution of funds after my mother's death to any of his children until I had my Ph.D. The will also contained a provision that ensured that I would have a place to live and enough money to complete my research. The situation was further complicated by the presence of my mother's older, unmarried sister, who had made her home with us for many years and had become totally blind the same week my father died. A warm and loving person accustomed to waiting on everyone in the household over the years, my aunt became almost completely dependent on others. Unfortunately, there were few who cared to help her.

I could fill you in on more details of the events in my life until June 1963, when I completed the Ph.D. Suffice it to say that I continued to drink heavily. A dry martini became my mainstay. My physical and mental lapses were noted by my brother, Tom, who had entered the AA program a year earlier. Tom was my favorite sibling. He was tall and handsome, and possessed a fine mind and athletic ability. In high school he had played on the basketball team that won the state championship. In 1942, he played varsity basketball on his Ivy League team while still a freshman. His favorite drink was milk until he discovered alcohol when he joined the service in 1944. Tom would casually leave AA pamphlets around my apartment and talk about meetings he attended. He never humiliated me, but eventually took me to AA meetings. He dragged me along to meetings in New York City and Connecticut, which led me to seek out meetings closer to home in New Jersey.

After completing my dissertation, I settled back in my hometown and undertook the care of my aunt. None of my brothers or sisters would take on the responsibility. At the time, my academic mentor was helping me find a teaching position. He submitted my academic records to prestigious universities in northern New York and the Midwest. But I chose not to pursue the positions because I didn't want to leave my aunt behind or move her to a new state. One of my sisters said that if I had been accepted at one of the schools she would have found a home for my aunt. But I never took her up on her offer.

Instead, I began teaching at the local campus of a private university in New Jersey in the mid-60s. I started as a substitute for a faculty member who was on maternity leave. I stayed on permanently, advancing from instructor to assistant professor by the end of the decade. During that period, the dean of the liberal arts college of the university appointed me dean of one of the college's three campuses. He had big plans for me. He was grooming me to take over at the university's overseas campus in England. He had no idea I was an alcoholic. I never made it to England. The dean was removed from his position by the president of the university. So instead of going to England, I returned to full-time teaching. I was relieved. I think my higher power acted on my behalf. You see, I didn't think I was up to the task. I was drinking a lot and would probably have gotten to England and collapsed from stress.

The dean may not have noticed anything unseemly in

my behavior caused by my drinking, but I learned later that some students did. I was told that they reported me to school administrators. Above all, I became frightened by what I knew were blackouts. One Sunday afternoon in the fall of 1969, as I was preparing a lecture for the following day, I said to myself, "If I don't stop drinking, I'm going to die." But I continued to have my two martinis before hopping in my car and driving to the college to teach my evening courses. In early December, I followed this routine for the last time. I remembered nothing until I woke up about 1:00 A.M. the following morning in my nightgown in my own bed. I could not recall how, or if, I got to campus. When I checked my car that morning, it was in its assigned parking space behind my apartment building. I don't know if I even gave a lecture, or how I got home. I do know that I received flowers from students in that class when I came home from rehab a few weeks later. I called my family doctor at 7:00 A.M. and told him what had happened. I also told him there were two places I knew for treatment of alcoholics; one was a five-day drying out place and the other was a lodge in northern New Jersey where the stay was usually much longer. He said five days would not do, and told me to call the lodge.

My decision to call the lodge and surrender to my alcoholism was prompted by the realization that I could not treat my problem alone. Attending AA meetings simply wasn't enough. I had read about the need of some alcoholics to move away, or be removed from, damaging situations. By the end of 1969, I was exhausted. I could no longer handle a full, four-course teaching load at the university, come home every day to prepare lunch for my aunt, and then return to the apartment at night to feed and care for her. Looking back, I don't know how I did it. My only escape was traveling abroad at the end of each summer. I went to Europe twice and Canada and South America once. My sister in Pennsylvania would take care of my aunt while I was out of the country. However, the one summer I traveled in the United States, my sister called me within forty-eight hours to complain about my aunt. As a result, the director of the lodge and my physician insisted that my aunt be sent to my sister in Pennsylvania for the duration of my stay at the rehab. Moreover, before she released me, the director arranged for my aunt to be removed from my apartment and eventually settled elsewhere.

My twenty-eight day stay at the lodge succeeded in teaching me to stay away from alcohol. The odds of getting better were stacked in my favor. A nurse at the lodge said that since I was a teacher, my chances of responding to the repeated teaching sessions at the rehab were better. I had also surrendered to my addiction before arriving at the lodge, having taken the first three steps of the AA program prior to checking in. And as the daughter of a doctor, I accepted my alcoholism because I viewed it as a disease. This acceptance was the most important factor in my recovery. Even today there are professionals in the health-care field who do not see alcoholism as a disease, but rather as a moral problem, a failure in self-discipline.

Before departing for her vacation in Florida, the lodge director told me that I would be released in mid-January 1970. She and the staff felt that I understood my alcohol addiction well enough to go back to, and survive in, the real world. The director's approval did wonders for my self-esteem, but I was still very, very shaky.

Many of the women being treated at the lodge speculated about whether or not they would lose their jobs when they returned to work. I had no idea what my fate would be. The lodge director advised me to say as little as possible about my disease and told me never to say that I was an alcoholic. Her strategy proved effective. Good timing helped me, too. My stay at the rehab coincided with the Christmas holiday and break between semesters at the university, making my absence less visible. My family doctor also wrote a letter to the chairman of my department and the dean, describing in correct medical terms my illness and stay at the rehab without once using the word "alcoholic." Meanwhile, one of my colleagues prepared my final exams for the fall term courses, and read and corrected them along with the term papers I had assigned.

I returned to the classroom and resumed a full teaching load at the end of January 1970. I was very vulnerable both physically and emotionally, but survived the spring semester intact, thanks to the tools of AA and new coping skills I learned at the rehab. I turned over to my higher power, whom I choose to call God, what then seemed to be problems I could not handle or control. I eventually found a sponsor and attended at least four meetings a week. I avoided meetings held in my hometown and county because of my professional occupation and that of my father, who had been a respected surgeon in the area. Instead, I drove to day and evening meetings twenty miles away. I continued to do so until the oil crisis of 1973, when I ceased the longer trips. I have stopped attending evening meetings altogether because of the danger a woman driving alone faces on the public highways today. In retrospect, I can see that such actions kept me sober. Indeed, my first five years in the program were relatively carefree. An old-timer warned me about the danger of remaining on "cloud nine" too long.

I believe my mental obsession with alcohol is far more powerful than my physical need for a drink. Although I would lick my lips when I saw others enjoying a cocktail or a glass of wine, after about a year, I began to serve alcohol beverages when I entertained in my apartment. Of course, I always kept an alcohol-free drink for myself. Once a guest noticed that my glass of "wine" was different from his. My answer, which conformed to the advice I received at the rehab and in AA, satisfied him. To this day, I always give away any alcohol remaining after a party to friends or family.

The 1970s had its triumphs and tragedies. I did well academically, advancing from assistant professor to associate professor, and then to full professor by 1975. The difficulties of the decade included the death of my aunt at the age of eighty-nine in a home for the blind. I have had three operations on my eyes for detached retinas, the same problem my aunt had endured for years. While the single operation performed years ago on one of her eyes did not restore her sight, mine succeeded, although imperfectly in one eye. Whereas the blackout of December 1969 was the turning point in my acceptance of my alcoholism and search for its treatment, the problem with my eyesight was the decisive factor in the termination of my teaching career and ultimate retirement in 1984.

My obsession for complete control twice reached dangerous proportions before my retirement. Against my sponsor's advice, I felt confident enough to tell one of my favorite colleagues at the university that I was an alcoholic. He was never the same afterward. He never again asked me to join a number of important committees he formed to improve the academic quality of our department. When a new university administration requested a review of the files of all faculty members, the new dean called me in and asked me about a notation made by the dean at the time of my heavy drinking and blackouts. In effect, the new dean said that if my unseemly behavior continued, I would be dismissed. When I replied that I was an alcoholic, but had been in AA for a long time, she seemed genuinely surprised. She said she admired me for admitting my problem. While the former dean never used the word, and to my knowledge kept it to herself, she chose to inform her closest associates in the university of my disease. University officials never treated me with the same respect afterward.

I had many choices in life, but too often made the wrong ones. Perhaps the most significant choice I ever made was not to keep in touch with my doctoral mentor when I began to look for a teaching job. He told me as much at a reception in his honor toward the end of his life. He thought well of my ability, even though I had been awarded the doctorate so late in life. My fear of being unable to achieve my goals kept me from recognizing his honest assessment of my work. As my sister said so long ago, if I had been accepted at any one of the institutions my mentor proposed, a family member would have found a place for my aunt. But I was an alcoholic and my disease would have impacted my life no matter where I taught. It might have even destroyed it.

I have an incurable, but treatable disease. Alcoholism is a physical, mental, and spiritual affliction. In my drinking days, I was totally irresponsible. If I did not like the consequences of my actions, I would simply walk away from them. There was always my father's safety net of material and emotional support. I was one of five children, but none of my brothers or sisters was so dependent. In the end, I came to recognize that my father was also dependent on me, for neither of his sons, on whom he lavished the best college education the nation offered, became a physician or business success. I think the provisions of his will resulted from his desire to have a professional—a doctor—in the family. Even though I was not to become an M.D., I was bright enough to earn a degree that would allow me to be called doctor. If not for my success, all of my father's hopes and dreams would have turned to dust.

Of course, they almost did. When I first read my parents' wills, I was angry. I said to myself: "Here I am the one child who did everything he asked, always lived up to his standards, and now even after his death, I still have to perform." To my surprise, none of my brothers or sisters sought to break the will. A well-loved AA member who was a lawyer once told me that I could have, and should have, broken the will. He thought my life would have been much happier had I done so. In retrospect, I'm glad I didn't.

With the help of God and AA, I shall celebrate my seventy-eighth birthday soon. Acceptance of my own defects and those of others has brought me this far.